Happy Leprechaun

Color in this picture using your crayons or colored pencils.

Let's Count!

Count the four-leaf clovers, leprechauns, horseshoes, boots, and hats.

Match the Cards

Can you find the two cards that are exactly the same?

SEEING DOUBLE

Two of these leprechauns are twins. Can you find and circle them?

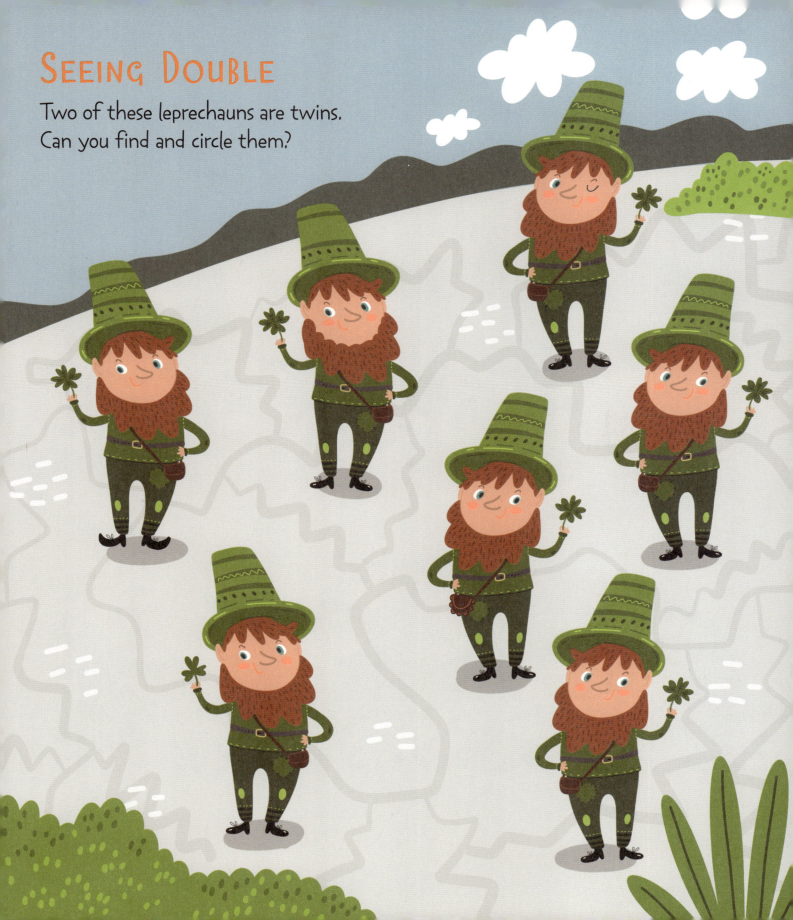

Pick a Hat

Trace the lines to see which hat belongs to each friend.

Counting coins!

Follow the maze to the pot of gold. Be sure to pass by the numbers 1–37 in order!

Happy Leprechaun

Color in this cheerful leprechaun using the color guide on the picture.

Holiday Math

Count each group of objects. Write the symbol for greater than (>), less than (<), or equal to (=) in the box on each line.

Match the Coins

Draw a line between the coins that are exactly the same.

GO FOR THE GOLD

You'll need one die, and each player will need a coin or other small object. Player 1 rolls the die and moves that many spaces on the board. If the player lands on a boot, move one more space forward. If the player lands on a hat, they lose a turn. If the player lands on a coin with a ladder, they follow it up, and if they land on a coin with an arrow pointing down, they follow it down. The first to reach the pot of gold wins!

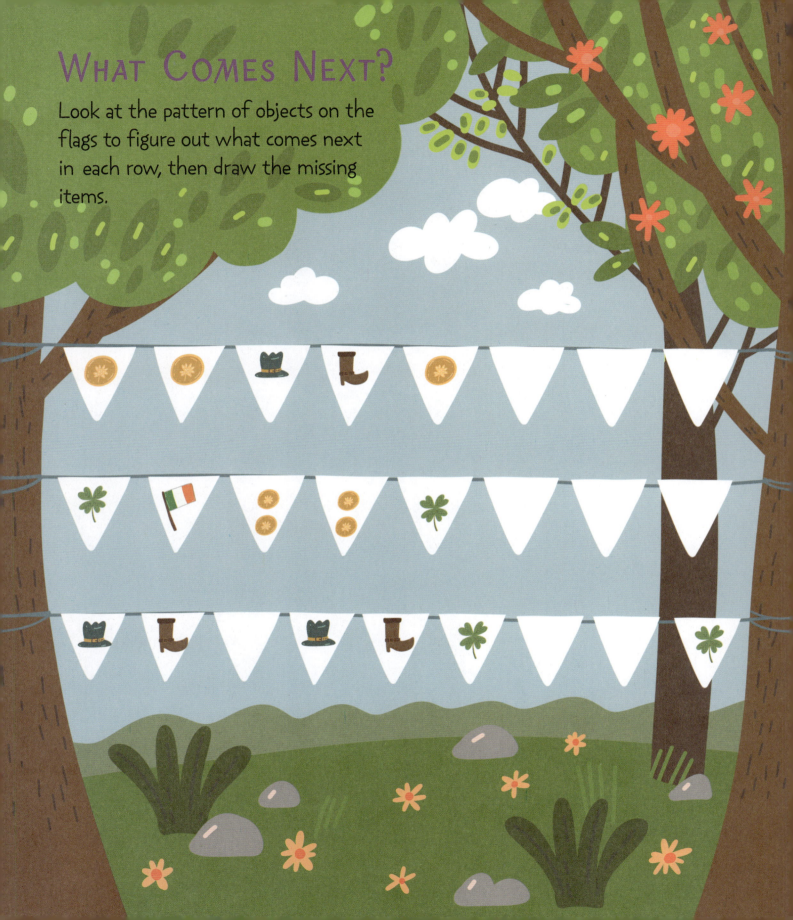

MAKE A WISH!

Carefully tear out this page from your book. Write down your biggest wishes. If you're patient, they just may come true!

Picture Puzzle

Cut out the small pieces below. Then glue them onto each puzzle so that there is only one of each object going up and down and across. (Tip: You might want to place all of the pieces first before gluing!)

Mystery Picture

Color in the squares using the key below.
Who is it?

Find the Differences

How many differences can you find between these two pictures?

HOLIDAY BEST

Johnny and Ginny are getting ready for a St. Patrick's Day party. Color their clothes any way you want to help them look their best!

Find the Differences

Can you find the 15 differences between these two pictures? Circle them as you find them.

Four-leaf Clover

Hold a pencil or colored pencil in each hand. Try to draw each side of the clover at the same time with both hands, following the direction of the arrows. Take your time and see how it turns out!

Spring Fair

Look carefully at the St. Patrick's Day Fair booths. Which two have all of the same objects?

Portrait Gallery

Color in these portraits and give each character a name!

GOLD COINS AND RAINBOWS

Color in this picture according to the color key.

Cat Leprechaun Twins

Look at all these cat leprechauns! Two are exactly the same. Can you find them?

FIND THE WAY TO GOLD

Can you help the cat find a way through the maze to the pot of gold? Be sure to collect the clovers and coins on the way!

START

FINISH

SHADOWS

Now look at these shadows of the dancers. Can you match each one to the pictures on the previous page?

PUZZLE

Can you figure out where these puzzle pieces go? Look carefully—one piece doesn't belong in the puzzle!

St. Patrick's Day Word Search

Find the words below in this puzzle. Words can be across, up and down, or diagonal in any direction!

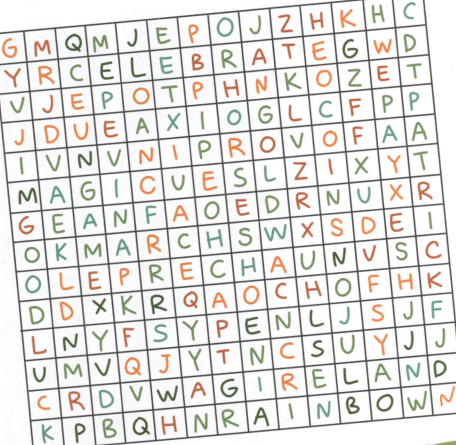

- POT
- PIPE
- LEPRECHAUN
- PATRICK
- CLOVER
- MARCH
- HAT
- MAGIC
- CELEBRATE
- GOOD LUCK
- COINS
- GREEN
- HORSESHOE
- GOLD
- RAINBOW
- IRELAND

Greeting Cards

Cut out each card along the dotted lines. Color in the pictures, then fold the cards in half along the solid line in the middle. Don't forget to sign your cards!

Leprechaun Word Search

Find the words in each puzzle and circle them. Words can be across, up and down, or diagonal in any direction. The words could be in either puzzle!

CELTIC IRELAND
CLAY PIPE LEPRECHAUN
CLOVER MARCH
DANCES MUSIC
EMERALD GREEN
　　　　HARP

F	G	O	D	N	A	L	E	R	I
O	T	L	D	E	R	A	S	G	S
P	O	L	E	M	E	L	O	N	N
H	G	A	L	E	C	D	T	E	E
A	N	I	L	L	T	I	N	R	G
R	G	H	P	C	I	A	S	E	L
O	E	S	A	T	R	O	N	P	R
A	G	N	U	N	U	A	H	C	E
D	D	A	A	C	I	M	U	S	I
H	C	R	A	M	R	U	L	C	C

H	A	S	H	O	E	M	E	P	A
C	R	P	R	E	K	A	D	A	R
L	A	E	P	C	L	O	V	E	R
D	Y	P	I	Y	R	T	E	O	R
A	N	T	R	E	F	O	I	L	P
K	C	E	S	W	H	D	R	U	W
N	S	E	S	H	I	S	D	I	O
O	P	R	S	A	T	T	H	A	B
T	E	N	T	M	E	O	P	T	N
W	O	R	K	R	O	C	K	R	A

ORANGE　　SHAMROCK
PARADE　　SHILLELAGH
POETRY　　SHOEMAKER
POT OF GOLD　SONGS
RAINBOW　　TOP HAT
SERPENTS　　TREFOIL
　　　　WHITE

Mystery Picture

Color in the boxes according to the color key. What do you see?

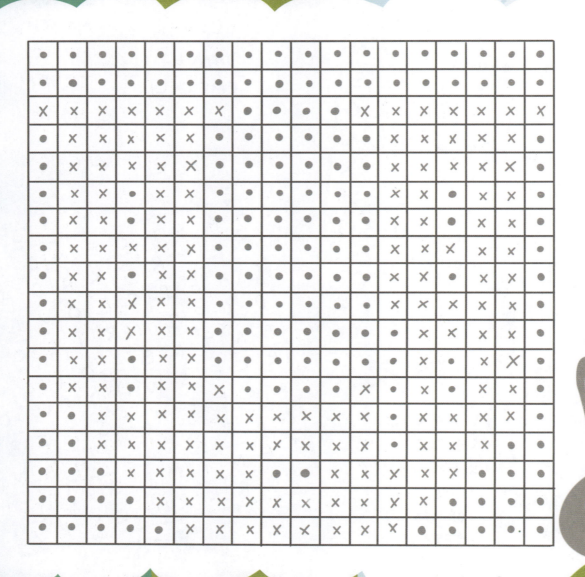

One, Two, Three...
Count the objects and write the numbers in the boxes below.

Clover Maze

Help the caterpillar find a way through the maze to the gold coin.

St. Patrick's Day Bookmarks

Color the pictures using your crayons or colored pencils. Carefully cut along the dotted lines to make your bookmarks!